# MY NAME IS RYAN

## I Am Just Like You
## but Different...

By
Ryan Walker Tidwell

and

Ryan's Nana, Beth McLemore Brock

# DEDICATION

## Beth:

Thanks to Ryan for being the awesome person he is, and for teaching us all a little patience and humility. Thanks to my daughter and son-in-law, his awesome parents, who didn't ask for this journey, but are navigating it with love and humor. Thanks to my son and his family, and my other grandchildren, who have never resented changing family plans because it is "easier for Ryan." Thanks to my husband, who always believes in me, and for the rest of my family and friends for their patience, confidence and encouragement. You will never know how much you are loved. Hugs and Kisses!! Ryan's Nana

## Ryan:

Thanks to Mom, Dad and my big brother, Brandon, for taking such good care of me. Thanks to my Nana and Pa who couldn't love me any more than they do. Thanks to my Uncle Robert, Aunt Jill, and my cousins for treating me like a normal kid. Thanks to my nurses – past and present – Paula, Sheena and Skyler – you are awesome – "Everything is Awesome when you are part of a team" – *The Lego Movie*. Love, Ryan

Nothing is impossible,
the very word says
"I'm possible!"

AUDREY HEPBURN

Hi. My name is Ryan.
I have brown hair and brown eyes.

Find the volume and surface area

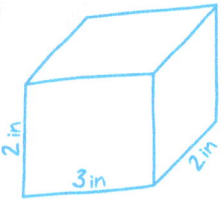

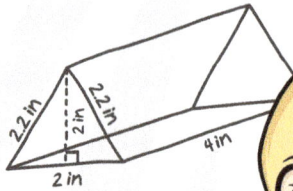

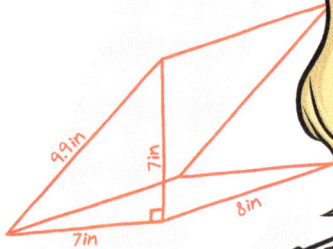

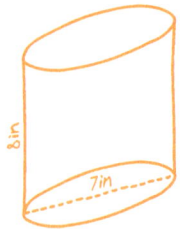

I'm 11 years old, and
I'm in the 6th grade.

I'm just like you...
but different.

Hi. My name is Ryan.
I love to play baseball,

but I'm better at bowling.

I love to
watch hockey,

football,

baseball,

and basketball
on TV.

I love the PS3, but I like the WII better.
I can beat my Nana at most games.

I'm just like you...
but different.

Hi. My name is Ryan.
I have a big brother and a
mommy and a daddy, grandparents,
and uncles and aunts and cousins.

I have two dogs,
a great family and
lots of friends.

I love playing outside and
going to the movies.

I'm just like you...
but different.

Hi. My name is Ryan.
My mommy says when I was born
I was the biggest baby in the nursery.

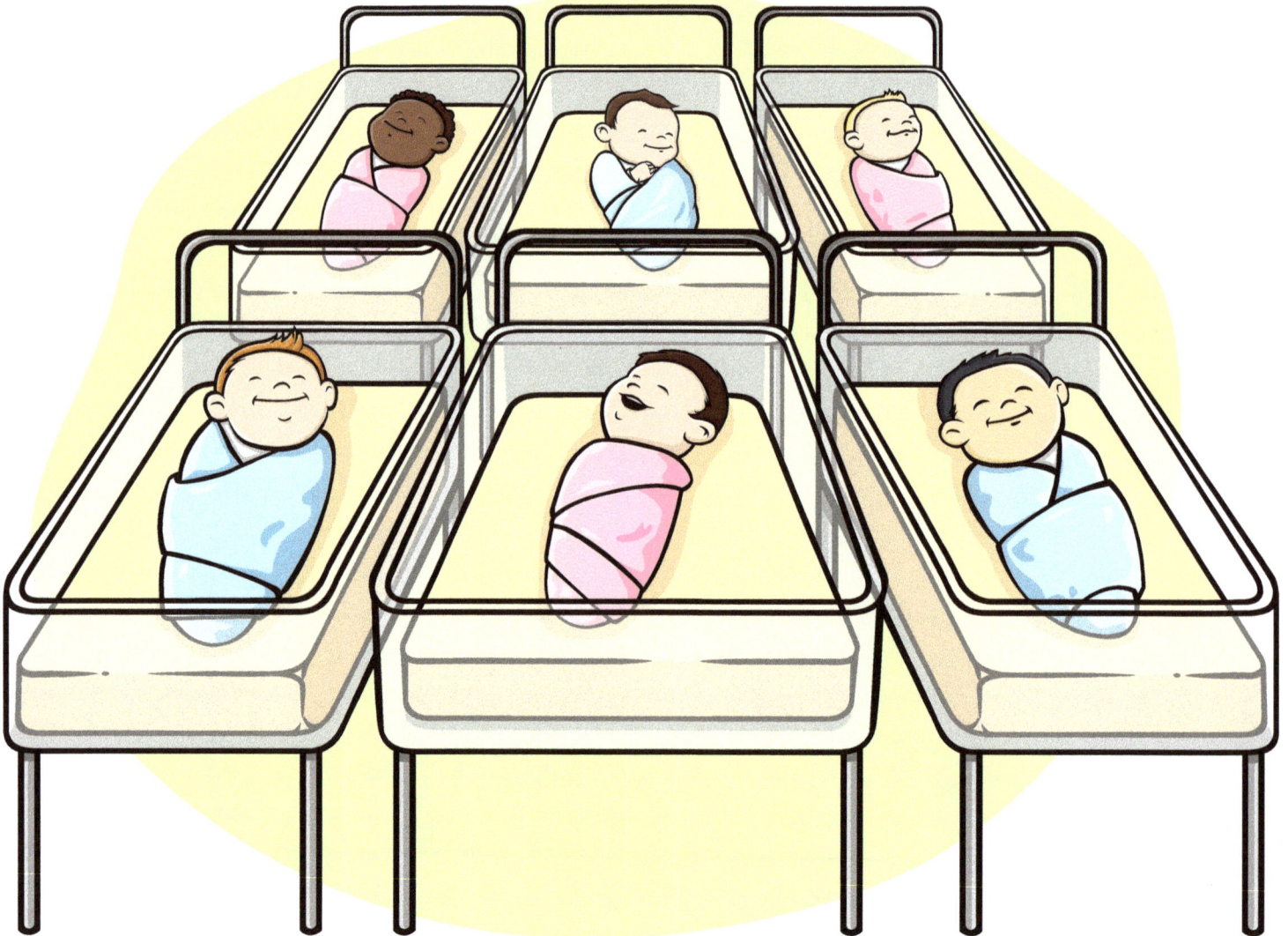

I was born with a hole in my back,
a problem with my eye, and
trouble with my breathing.
I was just like all the other babies...
but different.

Since I was very little, I've had operations on my back, on my eye, and on my brain; I see lots and lots of doctors and nurses.

I can't run and jump and
swim and climb.
But I like the playground,
just like you.

I have a special chair with wheels,
and a machine to help me breathe.

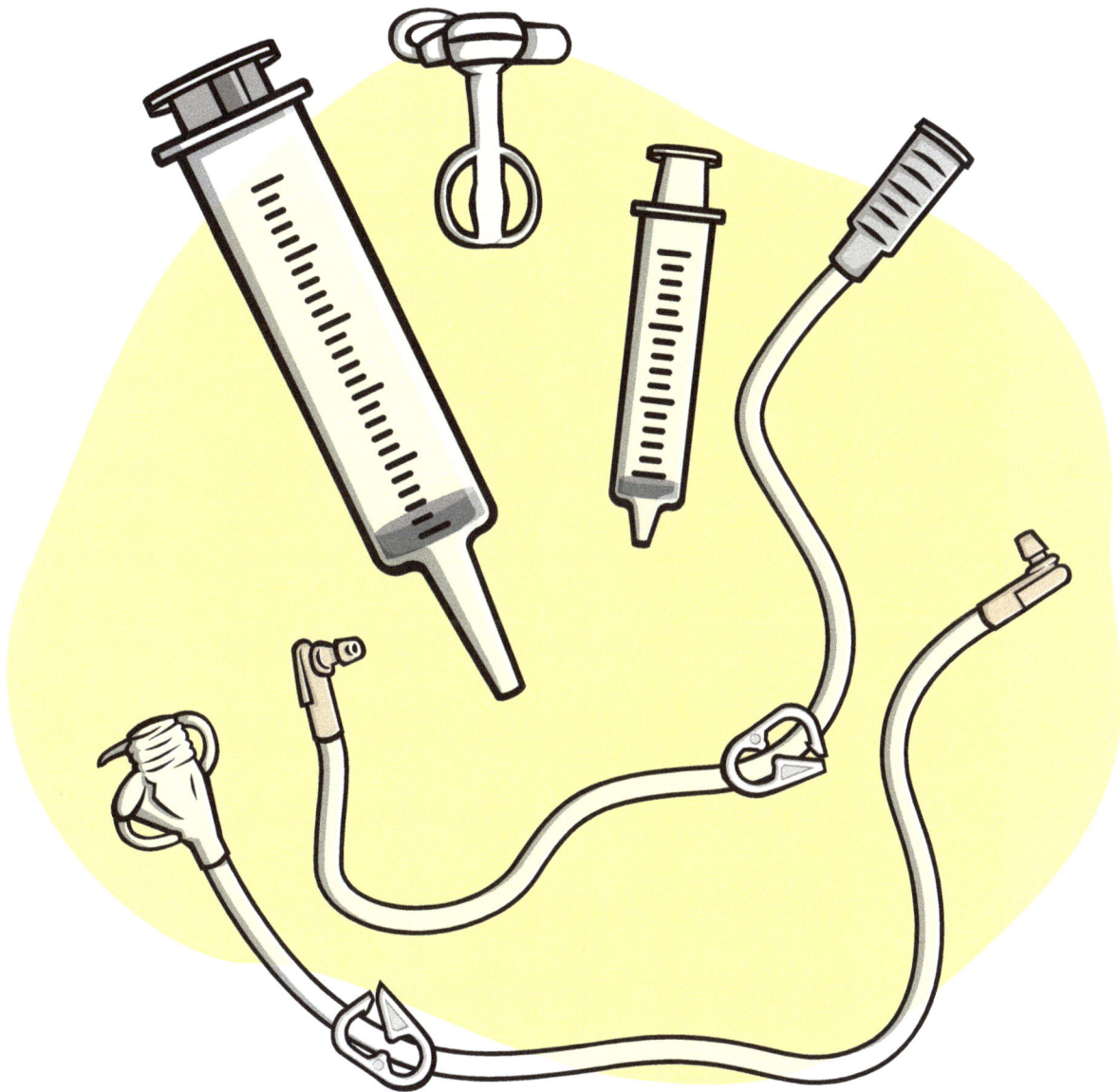

My food is given through a special tube, and
I have allergies, too.

I have a very special friend who is also a nurse.
She goes with me to school and helps me do everything!

She makes sure that I get to class on time
and do my homework, but
she also makes sure I get my rest.

I am just like you...
but different.

When I come home from school, I can't run and jump and play outside by myself, like you...

I have to have someone with me all the time.
Some kids are scared because of all my machines and
they don't talk to me even though I understand them.

I can also talk back to them, but sometimes they can't understand what I'm saying. I'm working on my **speech**.

Sometimes I get lonely.
I know that I'm different from all the other kids.

But, I'm still the same...
and my name is Ryan.

# ABOUT THE AUTHORS

## Beth:

Beth is new to the literary world. This is her first children's book, which was inspired by her special-needs grandson. She is a retired real estate paralegal; and in a former life taught ballet, tap and jazz to children. Beth lives outside Nashville, Tennessee with her husband and loves spending time with her grown children and grandchildren, who live close by. When she is not writing, she loves sewing, quilting and tap dancing.

## Ryan:

This is Ryan's first book, but you never know where this will lead. He is a student at Blackman Middle School in Tennessee. He is also active in C.A.P.E. (Challenged Athletes Playing Equally), supports Tucker's House, a non-profit, and participates in the Rutherford County, Tennessee Special Olympics thru school. He is always busy.

## Josh:

Josh Flanigan has been drawing since he could pick up a pencil, a sketchbook his constant companion growing up. A Western New York native, Josh studied illustration at Bryant and Stratton College and the Art Institute of Pittsburgh. He has worked as a graphic designer and illustrator since 1998 and currently works at Buffalo Spree magazine and is a contributor on Shutterstock.com. He has three children whom he adores and this project holds a place near and dear to his heart.

For information about this title or to order other books and/
or electronic media, contact the publisher:
Beth McLemore Brock
bethmclemorebrock@gmail.com

ISBN: 978-1-7323325-0-8 print
978-1-7323325-1-5 eBook

Printed in the United States of America
Cover and Interior design: 1106 Design
Illustrations by Josh Flanigan

www.ingramcontent.com/pod-product-compliance
Lightning Source LLC
Chambersburg PA
CBHW041600260326
41914CB00011B/1332